Centennial College
P.O. Box 631, Station A,
Scarborough, Ont.
M1K 5E9

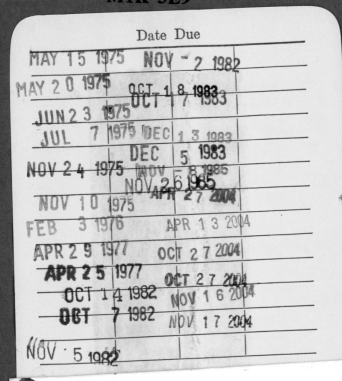

Nicholas Knock

Nicholas Knock

AND OTHER PEOPLE

POEMS BY DENNIS LEE

PICTURES BY FRANK NEWFELD

MACMILLAN OF CANADA

ISBN   0-7705-1194-5

OOKPIK

1963 mark and copyright of Her Majesty
the Queen in Right of Canada, used herein with
the permission of the Licensor and in association
with Noel J. Walsh and Associates, Exclusive
Canadian Licensee for OOKPIK publications.

The author is grateful to the Canada Council,
whose support helped him complete this book.
He is also grateful to the many people—
strangers and friends, young and old—who
contributed to the final form of the poems.

*

Two of the poems in this book, *The Coat* and
The Difficulty of Living on Other Planets,
appeared in an earlier publication, *Wiggle to the
Laundromat*, published by New Press. We are
grateful for permission to reproduce them here.

THIS BOOK WAS DESIGNED
BY FRANK NEWFELD

PRINTED AND BOUND IN CANADA
BY THE HUNTER ROSE COMPANY

The Macmillan Company of Canada Limited
70 Bond Street, Toronto M5B 1X3

Contents

6

Ookpik and the Animals

1

Ookpik came to see the zoo.
Ookpik had a thing to do.

He saw the lion in its cage;
Its eyes were full of sulky rage.

He watched the monkey, bored and glum,
Swinging like a pendulum;

And in another cage, he saw
The polar bear that sucked its paw.

Ookpik had a thing to do.
Ookpik marched around the zoo.

One cage held a jaguar.
Ookpik hopped on an iron bar;

He spun a little; he whirled alot;
He danced until the bar grew hot—

Until the bar grew hot and hotter,
Gave off steam like boiling water,

Sizzled like an iron welt—
And then the bar began to melt

And wobble with a twangy sound
Till it fell down flat on the dirty ground,

And soon the cage was in debris—
The jaguar was roaming free!

But Ookpik had a thing to do:
At the lion's cage, around he flew,

Around he spun like a top, zigzag
Until the bars began to sag

And the lion leaped through the burning air!
And then the monkey! and then the bear!

And soon the whole resounding zoo
Was dancing off in retinue

Behind the tiny whirling form
Of Ookpik (who was barely warm).

The wolf danced out with the antelope
And the python twirled like a skipping rope,

The spotted deer and the kangaroo,
The ocelot with the nosy gnu—

They danced right out of town, and then
They turned and danced back in again.

They stopped the cars; they jammed the street;
They danced in pairs on the raw concrete,

Panthers prancing, parrots loud,
Lambs and leopards through the crowd

Till off they frolicked, intertwined,
And left the city far behind.

Ookpik had a thing to do:
Ookpik danced away the zoo

And that's a thing I won't forget.
(For all I know, they're dancing yet.)

Going Up North

I'm going up north and live in the bush
Cause I can't stand parents that nag and push!

I'm going up north and live in a shack,
So tell my parents that I'm never coming back!
And I won't write letters,
    But I think I'll take a snack.

I'm going up north and I'll see strange sights.
I'll be all on my own with the Northern Lights.
I shall whistle to myself
    When the grizzly bears prowl,
And they'll say to one another
    As they snuffle and growl,
"I think I hear a tea kettle
    Coming to the boil,
Or maybe it's a radio
    That's going for a stroll,
Or an operatic porcupine
    Practising a role;
Imagine that—a porcupine
    Practising a role!"
Then the bears will start to fidget
    As they're lolloping along,
Cause a porcupine's ferocious
    If you interrupt his song;
And they'll mutter back and forth,
    "This is not the place for me—
I don't *want* to eat a porcupine—
    I think it's time to flee!"
And I'll squeak a sort of «YES!»
    And I'll maybe whistle less
And they'll never even guess
    That it's me.

Then I'll sneak back home in the dark of night
And I'll see my parents taking fits with fright
And I won't say Sorry,
    Or, Glad to be back,
But I'll give them a squeeze
    And quickly remark,
"What *marvellous* weather
    We're having today!

Did anything happen
While I was away?
The grizzlies were great;
And oh, by the way,
I hope you'll be nicer
Than yesterday."

Forty Mermaids

If I were swimming
In the sea
And forty mermaids
Came to me

And every mermaid
Wore a sign
Inviting me
To come and dine

With ocean heroes
Steeped in fame,
Like Captain Kidd
And What's-his-name,

And if the banquet
Hall were spread
With deep-sea ale
And ocean bread

And all the plates
Were living shells
That floated by
On tidal swells

And waiters wore
Their fin and tails
And served us each
A pinch of snails

And then dessert
Arrived in bubbles
And everyone
Was having doubles,

I think I'd stay
An hour or two
Before I swam
Back home to you.

He can whistle and dance on the walls.
He can dance on Niagara Falls.

    Like a fib in a sieve, like a wish
    Like a smile in a styrofoam dish

    Like an eel, like an ale, like an ark
    Like a muscle that sings in the dark

    Like a snail in a trance, like a flare
    Like an acrobat turning to air

He dances from morning to night.
Then he blinks. That turns out the light.

Attila the Hun
Is eating a bun
    At the corner of Yonge and Bloor.
I tell him, "Behave!
Now go get a shave!"
    But he pushes me down in the sewer,
The boor,
    And saunters up Yonge Street, cocksure.

A saint with a glare
And a mountain of hair
    Keeps crying "Repent!" in the park.
He looks like a hermit.
He hasn't a permit,
    And he won't even stop when it's dark:
Queen's Park
    Is no place for a saint after dark.

Rasputin the Monk
Is dancing, dead drunk,
    On the top of the New City Hall.
I've called for a cop.
I've begged him to stop,
    But he will not stop dancing at all—
The gall!
    If he doesn't stop dancing, he'll fall.
You can't *dance* on a New City Hall!

Mister Hoobody

There's a grubby sort of fairy
With the manners of a pig;
He isn't very little
And he isn't very big.
He lives inside our
Furnace, and he
Guzzles and he
Grunts.
His name is Mister Hoobody.
I've only seen him once.

He sneaks around and
Teaches children
What a fairy's for:
If you've eaten too much candy,
He always brings you more;
And when you're reading late, he tells you
"Why not read all night?"
And he keeps a pile of dimes
For kids that bite.

He's fat and fun and famous
And he doesn't wash his socks;
He wears a furry parka, just in
Case the furnace stops.
He drinks an awful lot, I guess to
Keep his stomach clean,
And when your parents come
He can't be seen.

Once I peeked inside the furnace, while he
Barbecued his toes:
The flames were red and crackly
Like his famous glowing nose;
He flickered through the shadows
Like a whizz-bang in a well,
Then he grinned a crooked grin
And made a smell.

A burp, a bounce, a guzzle
From his tiny whiskey keg,
Then the chubby little rubbydub
Spun quickly on one leg
Till, speeding up, he vanished
Like the vapour from a jet—
And as he went he thumped his chest:
"They haven't caught me yet!"

I hope that
Mister Hoobody will
Come back soon again.
Suppose I bounce a ball too high
And bend a window pane,
Or else my pen starts leaking
On the carpet
Like a sieve—
I hope that Mister Hoobody
Remembers where I live!

There was a man who never was.

This tragedy occurred because

His parents, being none too smart,

Were born two hundred years apart.

A Martian with a mangled spear

Is stuffing tarts in my left ear.

If I turn off my hearing aid

Will I still taste the marmalade?

There are midgets at the bottom of my garden.
Every night they come and play on violins.
One is named Molly, and one is named Dolly
And one has diarrhea, and grins.

There are wombats in the bureau of my uncle
And they loll about and pelt him with sardines.
But they sob like anything, when the midgets start to sing
For it reminds them of their aunt in New Orleans.

And the beaver with the bagpipes in the basement
Is a boarder that I know would not be missed:
For he makes the wombats roar, when he ties them to the floor
And he tells them that the midgets don't exist.

A skeleton called Wellington
Lives in my dresser drawer
Though every time I open it
He's just a pinafore.

But when I close it, he becomes
A lonesome soloist,
And Wellington the Skeleton
Gets up and does the Twist!

I hear him shake and rattle, like
A living castanet.
I've memorized the sound, although
I haven't seen him yet—

Cause every time I open it
The light gets in once more,
And Wellington the Skeleton
Is just a pinafore.

O Wellington the Skeleton,
We both know you exist:
Why won't you come outside and do
The living breathing Twist?

I know that I'm alive, and you
Are dead as dead can be:
But a skeleton gets lonely in a
Dresser, just like me.

And as for me, I figure I'll
Be bony too one day.
Why don't we get together, while
We still have time to play?

The Thing

Why do we walk every street, every block,
And stop all the people in turn,
Saying please, if you spot the Thing-Which-Is-Not,
Will you beg it for us to return?

Take pity on three who will never be free
Till we've told you the tale of our wrong.
The story is gory, and scary, and hoary—
I'll try not to make it too long:

Without a coat, without a hat,
Without a head it came;
The Thing! the Thing! the fearsome Thing
That followed and called us by name.
By the holes that reeked in its bleeding cheeks
We guessed that the Thing was blind,
But I had a knife, and Jim had a frog,
And Matt had a very good mind.

It had no feet, no shins, no knees—
We figured the Thing was lame;
But it followed us hard through a dozen backyards
Till up to our hideout it came.
Then I gave a gulp, and Jim turned to pulp
And Matt shut his eyes in alarm
For we saw, as it elbowed its way through the wall,
That the Thing didn't even have arms!

The Thing! the Thing! it started to sing,
It warbled! it babbled our names!
Then, leaping and snorting and clapping its hands,
Straight into the hideout it came!
I dodged to the left, Matt and Jim hung a right
And we raced to the end of the street
And there we looked back with a near heart attack
For the Thing was beginning to eat—

And what to our petrified eyes should appear
As the Thing went on munching apace?
It was eating its very own stomach, and wearing
A satisfied smile on its face.
And I was sick, and Jim was sick
And Matt made a bit of a mess;
But then we took off, for the Thing gave a cough
And it wheezed down the street after us.

We tore through the city, and it was a pity
To see six little legs flying.
But always behind us the Thing would remind us
Of unwelcome methods of dying.
So on we careened till we reached a ravine
Where Matt said it might have appeared
And we made for the grave at the end of the paving
And waited for It to draw near.

But the Thing went on shedding its body, like bedding,
By the light of the silvery moon;
One shoulder, a vest, thirteen ribs and the chest—
We saw there'd be nothing left soon.
So quick as a trice, Matt grabbed for the knife
And he waved it three times in the air
And cunning and brave, to the pit of the grave
He threw the knife down for a dare.

Then the Thing slithered in, with a sad little grin,
As though it had hoped to be friends,
And we pelted down dirt till our fingernails hurt
And we filled in the grave from both ends.
But sorry to say, and more sorry to tell,
When we opened the top of the cave
We had taken too long, and the Thing was all gone—
There was nothing at all in the grave!

Then Matt started crying: the Thing was just trying
To make friends with him, Jim and me,
And letting it die was a cowardly deed
For it merely had wanted to be.
So there, in the green of the gloomy ravine,
We cried for the wrong we had done:
Wherever we went, whatever we meant,
The Thing was eternally gone!

And that's why we walk every street, every block,
And we stop all the people in turn,
Saying please, if you spot a large Thing-Which-Is-Not,
Will you beg it for us to return?

(with Rachel Wyatt)

My mother took my hand in hers
And as she did she cried,
"You have my hair and eyebrows
But you have your Father's eyes."

I soaked them well in acid
To make them firm and round.
I love to see them wobble
As they roll along the ground.

My uncle on my mother's side
Was speechless in surprise:
"She has my teeth and fingernails
But she has her Father's eyes."

I scrubbed them with a toothbrush
Till they began to gleam.
I can't stand dirty eyeballs.
It makes me want to scream.

An aunt from Athabaska
Said proudly at the table,
"She has my ear, the right one.
I left it here last April."

Then turning to me sharply
She gave a vicious whack
And roared, "You have your
    Father's eyes,
For God's sake put them back!"

The enigmatic grundiboob
Adorns the icy Alps.
The purple people-eater hangs
His living room with scalps.
The Dreadful Snowman stalks the pole
In polar ecstasy:
But what a bore beside the lore
Of old Moose Factory!

The rubies in the Bagdhad roofs
Ignite the burning air.
The golden domes of Samarkand
Compose a fiery prayer.
The tinsel donnas of Madrid
Draw starfish from the sea:
Flashy trash, beside the lights
Of old Moose Factory!

Jack declared the Giant wasn't
Worth a hill of beans.
Samson flexed his armpits
And destroyed the Philistines.
Sir John A. built the CPR
With words and Scotch whiskey:
Pygmies all, beside the men
Of old Moose Factory!

1

If I could teach you how to fly
Or bake an elderberry pie
Or turn the sidewalk into stars
Or play new songs on an old guitar
Or if I knew the way to heaven,
The names of night, the taste of seven
And owned them all, to keep or lend—
Would you come and be my friend?

2

You cannot teach me how to fly.
I love the berries but not the pie.
The sidewalks are for walking on,
And an old guitar has just one song.
The names of night cannot be known,
The way to heaven cannot be shown.
You cannot keep, you cannot lend—
But still I want you for my friend.

A parking meter told me,
As on my way I went,
"You're ticking like a time bomb, but
Your heart is pure cement.

"You haven't got a dollar,
You haven't got a dime.
You haven't got a lousy match
To light your coal black mind."

I bowed three times, and thanked him twice,
And punched him in the nose,
Then beat him with a want-ad till he
Tore off all his clothes.

"Wait!" he cried, "I'm actually
A fairy in disguise.
I tempted you with gloomy thoughts,
To see if you were wise.

"You pass the little Sunshine test;
Now, here's your little wand —"
I picked him up and pitched him
In an ornamental pond.

I don't mind parking meters that
Get lippy now and then,
But I can't stand fairies going round
And doing good to men.

The Poodle and the Grundiboob

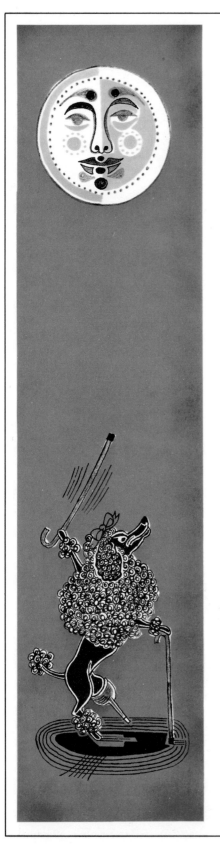

A poodle and a grundiboob
Were dining on the moon.
The poodle had a wooden leg,
The boob was born in June.

The only thing the poodle said
Was, "Give me back my spoon."
The boob had better manners; he
Gave thanks, and ate a prune.

The poodle shed a sable tear,
He cried, "My leg is loose."
The grundiboob expressed regret
And drank the poodle's juice.

The poodle couldn't slice the bread,
His leg was coming off.
The grundy ate the loaf entire
And gave a hungry cough.

Across the plates, across the chairs
The poodle chased the broth.
The grundy cheered him on, and then
Devoured the tablecloth.

The poodle roared, "Who ate the plate?
My three good legs all hurt!"
To comfort him, the grundy murmured,
"You can be dessert."

The poodle isn't hungry now
Although he hasn't dined.
The grundiboob just licks his lips.
The leg remains behind.

Oilcan Harry

Oilcan Harry, feeling bored,
Tied his sister to a Ford.
Harry chuckled at the gag.
Sister found it quite a drag.

Oilcan Harry used to cram
His brothers underneath the tram.
"Gosh," he grumbled, "Heaven sakes,
Why should they get all the breaks?"

Oilcan Harry never meant
To drown his dad to that extent:
He only kept him in the tank
Because the tar and feathers stank.

Oilcan Harry drew the line—
Up and down his uncle's spine.
He used sulphuric, I might say.
Uncle's spineless to this day.

The day she died, just on a hunch,
Harry had his mum for lunch.
Now he can't sit down to sup
Without bringing Mother up.

Oilcan Harry met his doom
Building bombs in the living room:
When he saw he'd made a goof,
Oilcan Harry hit the roof.

Curse:

On a Driver, Who Splashed His New Pants When He Could Have Just as Easily Driven Around the Puddle

May your large intestine freeze in a knot like a skate-lace!
May manhole covers collapse wherever you go.
May garbage strikes pester your street, and may you grow eight new
Feet and get poison ivy on every toe!

1

A senior wizard
Of high degree
With a special diploma
In wizardry
Is trudging along
At the top of the street
With a scowl on his face
And a pain in his feet.

A beard, a bundle,
A right-angle stoop,
And a cutaway coat
Embroidered with soup,
A halo of smoke
And a sputtery sound—
The only real magic
Magician around!

But nobody nowadays
Welcomes a wizard:
They'll take in a spaniel,
Make room for a lizard—
But show them a conjurer
Still on the ball,
And nobody wants him
Or needs him at all.

His bundle is bulging
With rabbits and string,
And a sort of machine
That he's teaching to sing,
And a clock, and a monkey
That stands on its head,
And a mixture for turning
Pure gold into lead.

He carries a bird's nest
That came from the Ark,
He knows how to tickle
A fish in the dark;
He can count up by tens
To a million and three—
But he can't find a home
For his wizardry!

For *nobody*, nowadays,
Welcomes a wizard:
They'll drool at a goldfish,
Repaint for a lizard,
But show them a magus
Who knows his stuff —
They can't slam their latches down
Quickly enough!

2 In Casa Loma
Lives a cat
With a jet-black coat
And a tall silk hat.
And every day
At half past four
He sets the table
For twelve or more.

The spoons parade
Beside each plate;
He pours the wine,
He serves the steak,
And Shreddies, and turnips,
And beer in a dish —
Though all he can stomach
Is cold tuna fish.

But a cat is a cat
In a castle or no,
And people are people
Wherever you go.

Then he paces about
In the big dining hall,
Waiting and waiting
For someone to call
Who won't be too snooty
For dinner and chat
At the home of a highly
Hospitable cat.

And every evening
At half past eight,
He throws out the dinner
And locks the gate.
And every night,
At half past ten,
He climbs up to bed
By himself, again.

For a cat is a cat
In a castle or no,
And people are people
Wherever you go.

3 One day they meet
In a laundromat,
The lonesome wizard,
The coal-black cat.

And chatting away
In the clammy air,
They find they both like
Solitaire,

And merry-go-rounds,
And candle-light,
And spooky yarns
That turn out right.

They stroll together
Chatting still
To Casa Loma
On the hill

And there the cat
Invites his friend
To share a bite,
If he'll condescend;

And, yes, the wizard
Thinks he might—
But just for a jiffy
And one quick bite.

An hour goes by
Like a silver skate.
The wizard moves
From plate to plate.

Two hours go by,
Like shooting stars.
The cat produces
Big cigars

And there in the darkening
Room they sit,
A cat and a wizard,
Candle-lit.

At last the wizard
Takes the pack
From his creaking, reeking,
Rickety back.

He sets it down
With a little shrug,
And pulls a rabbit
From under the rug.

And before you can blink
He's clapping his hands,
And there in the doorway
A peacock stands.

Now he's setting the monkey
Upon its head,
He's turning the silverware
Into lead

And counting by tens
From a hundred to four
And making a waterfall
Start from the floor

And juggling a turnip,
A plate and a dish,
And turning them all
Into fresh tuna fish.

The cat is ecstatic!
He chortles, he sails
From the roof to the floor
On the banister rails,

And soon the whole castle
Is whizzing with things:
With sparklers and flautists
And butterflies' wings,

And all through the night
The party goes on,
Till it stops in a trice
At the crack of dawn

And the wizard installs
His pack in a drawer,
While the cat tidies up
The living-room floor.

And as the sky
Is growing red,
They tiptoe up
The stairs to bed.

The wizard's snore
Is rather weird:
The cat is snuggled
In his beard—

Dreaming of tuna fish
End to end,
And rabbits, and having
A brand-new friend.

Perhaps you wonder
How I know
A cat and a wizard
Can carry on so?

Well, if some day
You chance to light
On Casa Loma
Late at night

Go up to the window,
Peek inside,
And then you'll see
I haven't lied.

For round & round
The rabbits dance,
The moon is high
And they don't wear pants;

The tuna fish
Patrol the hall,
The butterflies swim
In the waterfall

And high and low,
With a hullaballoo,
The castle whirls
Like a tipsy zoo.

And in the corner,
If you peer,
Two other figures
May appear.

One is dressed
In a tall silk hat:
The lord of the castle,
The jet black cat.

The other's a wizard
Of high degree.
The wizard is grinning.
The wizard is me.

The Lesser Glunk has two in front
And one behind, for when he's drunk.
The Speckled Stripes around his eyes
Are plain as day, unless he cries
(Alas, he is a Tearful Thing
And sobs at almost anything,
Such as the Root of πr^2,
Cab-drivers, Sober or Impaired,
The Bill of Rights, the Goal of Life,
And every kind of Mental Strife).

 The Male breathes In and Out all day
While Females breathe the other way,
Which ought to tell us Which is Who
Except they both maintain the View
That Breathing is a strict Taboo;
And that is why, when hunting Glunks,
One always carries extra Lunks.

 The Nose looks like an Ironing Board
But Isn't, so should be ignored
For Glunks wear Very Scanty Clothes
And seldom iron even those.
And watch his Famous Crested Trace
Which rarely lingers in one place
But Wanders, like a Tennis Ball,
And sometimes Isn't There At All.

 You'll know him by his Blasted Cheek,
His Rumpled Stare, his Warty Squeak—
But here's the surest clue of all:
A glunk Won't Answer when you call!
So if you can't hear anythink
You've seen a Lesser Glunk (I think).

The reason I clobbered
Your door like that,
Is cause it's time
We had a chat.

But don't start getting
Talkative—
I've got a speech
I want to give:

"A person needs
A pal alot,
And a pal is what
I'm glad I've got,

So thank you. Thank you."
There, it's said!
I feel my earlobes
Getting red,

And I wish you wouldn't
Grin that way!
It isn't healthy,
Night or day.

But even though
You're such a jerk,
With your corny jokes
And your goofy smirk,

I'm sort of glad
You're my old pard.
You're cheaper than
A bodyguard,

And smaller than a
Saint Bernard,
And cleaner than a
Wrecker's yard.

I like the way
You save on socks:
You wear them till they're
Hard as rocks.

And I think those missing
Teeth are keen:
Your mouth looks like
A slot machine

And every time
I see you grin,
I stick another
Quarter in.

You make me laugh
Till we trip on chairs;
One day we nearly
Fell downstairs.

But I think you're kind of
Brave, I guess:
Your no means no,
Your yes means yes,

And even if
It makes you shrink,
You say the things
You really think.

In fact your mouth
Is never closed—
Your tonsils blush,
They're so exposed.

And your tweety voice
Is never quiet;
They must put birdseed
In your diet.

Still, you seem to know,
When we kid alot,
A time for kidding
A time for not –

Cause often things
I say to you,
I'd ache if any
Body knew.

You choke me up,
You make me sneeze,
I've caught you like
A rare disease:

I'd like to come and
Rub your back;
I'd like to feed you
Crackerjack

And send you messages
In code
And walk along you
Like a road

And bath you till your
Fleas are gone
And stuff you like
A mastodon,

And let's go play
In Kendal Park;
There's still an hour
Before it's dark.

Cause some things last and
Some things end –
I want you always
For my friend.

Sparrows sniffed the air, and hung
Like humming-birds with bubble gum
Doing pushups in the sun
  The day we stopped Spadina.

The people stopped to touch the air
And breathe the green renewal there
As though the headline was a prayer
  The day we stopped Spadina.

And parking lots came out to play
Arrayed in green instead of grey
And I said, Why not stay that way?
  The day we stopped Spadina.

I watched a woman's face which glowed
I saw computer cards explode
And I heard grass grow on Walmer Road
  The day we stopped Spadina.

And Bishop Strachan from underground
Was half converted by the sound
Of pleasure in Toronto town
  The one and only day we stopped Spadina.

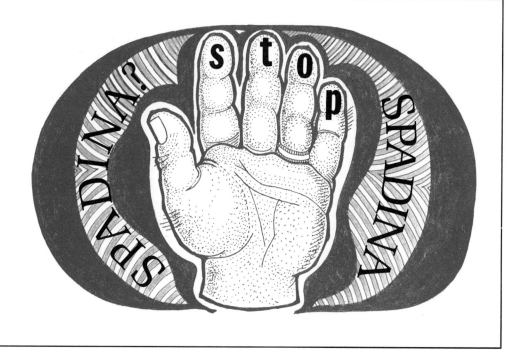

The Compact sat in parliament
To legalize their fun.
And now they're hanging Sammy Lount
And Captain Anderson.
And if they catch Mackenzie
They will string him in the rain.
And England will erase us if
Mackenzie comes again.

The Bishop has a paper
That says he owns our land.
The Bishop has a Bible too
That says our souls are damned.
Mackenzie had a printing press.
It's soaking in the Bay.
And who will spike the Bishop till
Mackenzie comes again?

The British want the country
For the Empire and the view.
The Yankees want the country for
A yankee barbecue.
The Compact want the country
For their merrie green domain.
They'll all play finders-keepers till
Mackenzie comes again.

Mackenzie was a crazy man,
He wore his wig askew.
He donned three bulky overcoats
In case the bullets flew.
Mackenzie talked of fighting
While the fight went down the drain.
But who will speak for Canada?
Mackenzie, come again!

Winter Song

I saw two crows upon a tree
Scrawking and cawing endlessly:
"Light on the leaves, and then goodbye.
What is the cold wind's alibi?"
    "I do not know," said I.

I saw the snow truck up the street,
Taking the slush from the curb to eat:
"Think of forsythia, last July—
Where are the petals that filled the sky?"
    "Ask me again," said I.

I saw a sparrow, small and alive,
Skipping for food in the snowy drive:
"Do we endure in God's great eye?
Is there a green that does not die?"
    "We'll wait and see," said I.

The Coat

I patched my coat with sunlight.
It lasted for a day.
I patched my coat with moonlight,
But the lining came away.
I patched my coat with lightning
And it flew off in the storm.
I patched my coat with darkness:
That coat has kept me warm.

The Saint's Lament

Come study the names
Of my trouble and ills:
Paradise fever
And salvation chills.

I gave up the dancing,
I paid all the bills,
And now I am sick with
The salvation chills.

The world is behind me,
The wild times are through—
But paradise fever
Has cut me in two.

An earthy man grins
As he gorges and swills,
But the righteous are stricken
With salvation chills,

For righteous men eat
And are not satisfied—
Paradise tastes
Like formaldehyde.

Those bodies are warm
In their beds where they lie.
I wish I lay with them.
I kissed them goodbye.

It's time to start over,
Alive though it kills;
Lord God, resurrect me
From salvation chills.

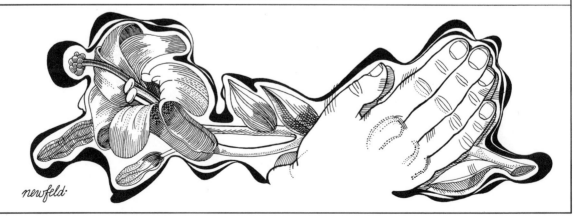

The light was free and easy then,
Among the maple trees,
And music drifted over
From the neighbours' balconies;
Half my mind was nodding
With the asters in their ranks,
And half was full to bursting
With a hungry kind of thanks.

It wasn't just the mottled play
Of light along the lawn.
I didn't hope to live back all the
Good times that were gone;
All I wanted was to let
The light and maples be,
Yet something came together as they
Entered into me.

And what was singing in my mind
Was in my body too:
Sun and lawn and aster beds
Murmuring, I do—
Earth, beloved, yes, I do I
Too am here by grace,
As real as any buried stone
Or any blade of grass.

Breath and death and pestilence
Were not revoked by that.
Heavy things went on, among
The calm magnificat.
Yet as I sat, my body spoke
The words of my return:
There is a joy of being, which you
Must be still and learn.

Part One

Nicholas Knock was a venturesome boy.
    He lived at Number Eight.
He went for walks in the universe
    And generally got home late.

But Nicholas Knock was always around
    When the ice-cream truck went *ching*.
He dug up flowers, to watch them grow
    And he mended them with string.

He found a chipmunk, shivering like a
    Fur-cube in the snow.
He nursed it through to the end of March
    And then he let it go.

Acres of grass and acres of air—
    Acres of acres everywhere:
The sun shone high, and the moon shone low
    And Nicholas didn't care.

So Nicholas Knock went doodling
    Through summer & winter & spring.
His mind had funny edges
    And the ice-cream truck went *ching*.

Part Two

One year it was Tuesday; Nicholas Knock
Went noodling off for a bit of a walk.
He hid on his brother; he raced a dog;
He helped a little kid catch a frog.
Then at the curb and walking east
He spied the silver honkabeest.

A trick, a flicker of the light;
The tiny creature, like a flight
Of warblers, seemed to ride the air
And shed a frisky lustre there.
And yet it did not move a hair.

Its eyes were dusky, deep, and clear.
It rose; it flew; it settled near
And Nicholas stood by its delicate side,
Nicholas stood and almost cried.

He left it then, but all that night
He dreamed of its radiant arc in flight.
And when he returned in the morning, the air
Was dimpled with light and the creature was there!
And every day, for a month at least,
He met the silver honkabeest.

Part Three

"O mother, dear mother
    Prepare us a feast;
I'm friends with the silver
    Honkabeest!

"Oh father come quickly,
    I want you to see
For it's shiny and gentle as
    Gentle can be."

"Nicholas Knock!"
    His parents hissed,
"That honkabeast
    Does not exist!"

But Nicholas whinnied,
    And Nicholas sang,
And Nicholas hopped
    Till his bell-bottoms rang.

"I've seen it! I've seen it!
    I'm practically sure:
We meet every morning
    At Brunswick and Bloor."

His parents sat down,
    Exchanging a glance—
Alas for their son
    With his weirdo dance!

Even the neighbours
    Were starting to talk:
What was the matter
    With Nicholas Knock?

His mother declared,
    "I wish I was dead!"
And all in a fury
    His father said,

"This neighbourhood
    Should be policed
To get that vicious
    Honkabeast!"

But Nicholas figured
    Their tempers would mend,
So Nicholas tore off
    To visit his friend.

Part Four

"Frisky, most silver, serene—
bright step at the margins of air, you
tiny colossus and
winsome and
master me, easy in sunlight, you
gracious one come to me, live in
my life."

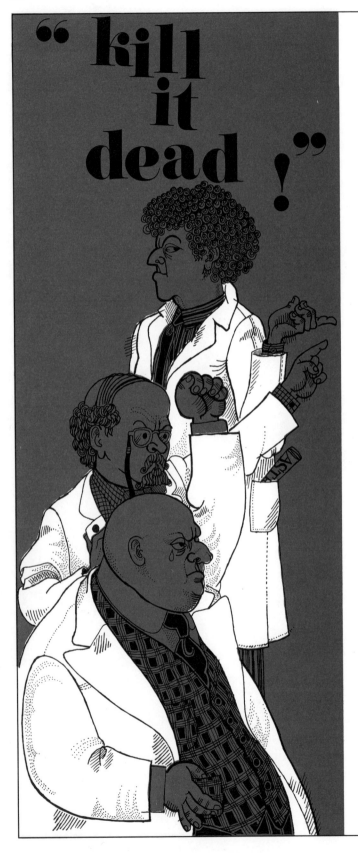

"kill it dead!"

Part Five

Well ~

They took him to
    A specialist
Who soon prescribed
    An oculist
And then a child
    Psychologist
And last a demon-
    Ologist,
Who knew about
    Astrology
And dabbled in
    Phrenology.

Their diagnoses
    Disagreed
But on one thing
    They all agreed:
If Nicholas Knock's
    Delusion ceased
(He thought he saw
    A honkabeast),
The boy would mend
    Within a year;
But otherwise
    His fate was clear—
A life in hospitals,
    Designed
To pacify
    The deviant mind,
A life in
    Institutions, meant
To exorcize
    Such devilment;
But still the boy
    Could be released
If he gave up
    His honkabeast.

Their words were kind,
    Their eyes sincere,
Their arguments
    Were strong and clear:
Because the honka-
    Beast was not,
He ought to kill it
    On the spot;
Because it was
    An utter fraud,
He ought to offer
    It to God.

Yet heartless, witless,
    Stubborn and slow,
Nicholas Knock
    Kept murmuring, "No."
They yelled at him,
    They shed real tears
Till Nicholas finally
    Plugged his ears;
The more they told him
    "Kill it dead!"
The harder Nicholas
    Shook his head.

At last they cried,
    "His time is short.
Take him away, to
    Supreme Court."

*

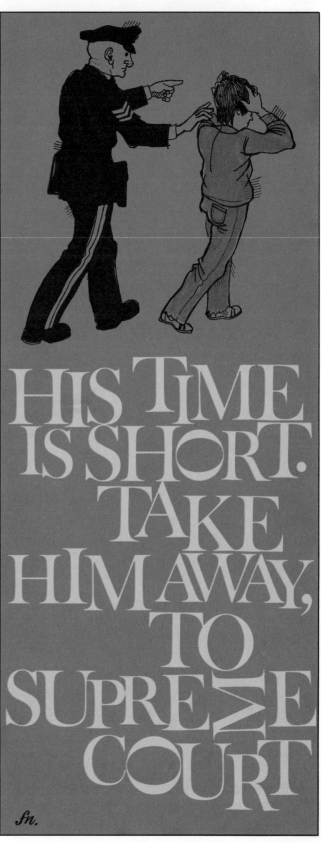

HIS TIME IS SHORT. TAKE HIM AWAY, TO SUPREME COURT

SILENCE!
POPPYCOCK
INSOLENCE
!

Part Six

Snort! went the
Court clerk, and
Pounded on the table-top.
"Stand!" cried the
Bailiff with a
Steely-eyed stare.
"Name?" shrilled the
Registrar, and
Poked him with a fountain-pen.
"Swear!" boomed the
Justice with a glare.

"Please," stammered
Nicholas, "I've seen the silver
Honkabeest—"
"Silence!" roared His
Lordship, "that's a
Rumour and a lie!
Poppycock and
Insolence! The
Honkabeast is *not* a beast—
How are we to know it's not a
Pervert, or a spy?
Eh?
It's probably a pervert *and* a spy.

"Unless you sign a declaration
That the honkabeast is fiction,
Then I must—as a precaution,
To preserve Confederation—
Place a legal limitation
On your circumambulation
With a minor operation
Which we call decapitation."

Nicholas, Nicholas
Nicholas Knock
Do what he says
Or you'll go to the block.

Nicholas, Nicholas
Living or dead
Sign what he says
Or they'll chop off your head.

Nicholas stood,
He quivered with fear,
As he uttered the words
Which I set down here:

"I'm frightened of burglars,
I shake in the dark,
And I'm scared of your sharp sharp knife;
But I love the silver
Honkabeest
More than I love my life.

"I will not sign your paper.
I will not sign your bill.
I've seen him every day for a month
And I hope I always will."

Nicholas Knock,
You'll soon be deceased—
Why should you die
For a honkabeest?

Part Seven

His Lordship was raging,
    He sputtered and said,
"Take out the rascal
    And chop off his head! –
And by midnight tonight
    There'll be two of them dead!

"For the army, the navy,
    The Mounted Police,
The bailiff, the sheriff,
    And I
Will personally go
    To the honkabeast's den,
Preparing to do
    Or to die.
With thousands of soldiers,
    And guns in each hand,
With bombers and
    Submarines –

To safeguard our children
    We'll blast it and blitz it
To billions of
    Smithereens!!
And at last this land
    Will be released
From the threat of the terrible
    Honkabeast!"

Now, Nicholas had
Listened with a
Very meek expression;
Nicholas had heard him
With a look of
Meek dismay.
But when His Lordship spoke about
The bombing
Of the honkabeest,
Nicholas's meekness seemed to
All
Go
Away.

"Thump!" went his
  Fist upon the
  Forehead of the clerk of court—
"Crack!" went his shoes against the
  Registrar's shin—
"Squelch!" as his head
  Hit the lawyer's bulgy
  Stomach, and—
"Sssmrtch!" as he caved His Lordship's
  Hearing-aid in.

Then Nicholas whizzed
    And Nicholas whanged
And Nicholas knocked
    Till their craniums rang.

He rolled them up in table-cloths,
    He dumped them in the sink,
He covered them with prune-juice
    Till their eyeballs ran like ink.
He hung them from the curtain-rods,
    He slathered them in foam
And told them, gently, "Leave the silver
    Honkabeest alone."
And then he pulled the ceiling down
    And made his way back home.

Part Eight

The sky was as blue as a clear blue sky,
    The sun was hot and high,
When Nicholas came with a flick in his step
    And a fidgety glint in his eye.

The city hung around him, like a
    Quick and dirty scrawl:
The traffic lights, the neon lights,
    And the Bank of Montreal.

He never looked to left or right;
    He came home straightaway
To where the silver honkabeest
    Had met him every day.

He watched the stores; he watched the cars;
    He spied a silver light
That winked at him, and blinked at him—
    And disappeared from sight!

And hunting round to find the thing
    He thought he heard a hoof
That clickered like a honkabeest's,
    But vanished without proof.

And here a snort, and there a tail,
    And silver without end:
He spent a day and night that way,
    But he couldn't find his friend.

But neither could he give it up
    (And this is what was queer),
For every time he started to,
    The thing would reappear.

And if you take a walk on Bloor
    You still can see a boy
Whose face is sometimes in despair
    And sometimes full of joy.

You'll see him stalk and whirl around
    A hundred times at least.
Don't bother him! He's hunting for
    A silver honkabeest.

A Song for Ookpik

Ookpik,
Ookpik
Dance with
Us,
Till our
Lives
Go
Luminous.

When the
Slush is
In the
Street,
Ookpik
Touch our
Soggy
Feet.

Feed the
Headlong
Green, in
Case
We do not
Leave it
Living
Space

Till the
Green
World
Gallivants
To the
Voltage
Of your
Dance.